THE PROMISE OF
KILIMANJARO

Golden sun reflected against the side of Kilimanjaro - taken
at an altitude of 13,000 feet, midway to the summit.

THE PROMISE OF
KILIMANJARO

Jay Scheiner

ISBN-13: 9781983998850
ISBN-10: 1983998850
Library of Congress Control Number:2017917922
CreateSpace Independent Publishing Platform, North Charleston, SC

To Carol, who understood

Contents

Forward · xiii

Kilimanjaro Map ·xiv

Introduction · xv

1   Questing · 1
2   Training · 11
3   Ascending· 19
4   Struggling · 49
5   Crossing · 61
6   Summiting · 73
7   Freefalling · 79
8   Descending · 89
9   Awakening · 95

Team Dirt's Timeline · 105

Acknowledgments · 107

Resources · 111

About the author · 119

Forward

By Joseph Jordan, author of
Living a Life of Significance

I HAVE KNOWN Jay Scheiner for years. All his life has been dedicated to helping others, from working as a drug enforcement agent to more than 20 years teaching boating safety courses. Jay's success in financial services is founded in his belief that serving others gives our lives meaning and purpose.

It wasn't until I read *The Promise of Kilimanjaro* that I realized Jay also has a seriously adventurous side. Jay's new book was a refreshing surprise to me as he takes us along on his harrowing adventure in Africa. The hero's journey, usually experienced through mythological tales from Beowulf to Star Wars, is played out in four parts: call to adventure, ordeal, resurrection, and return. Jay actually experienced all four of these stages during his ascent and treacherous descent of Kilimanjaro.

If you're up for a mythological thrill of human endurance coupled with the reality that a real person accomplished this journey, then *The Promise of Kilimanjaro* is a must read!

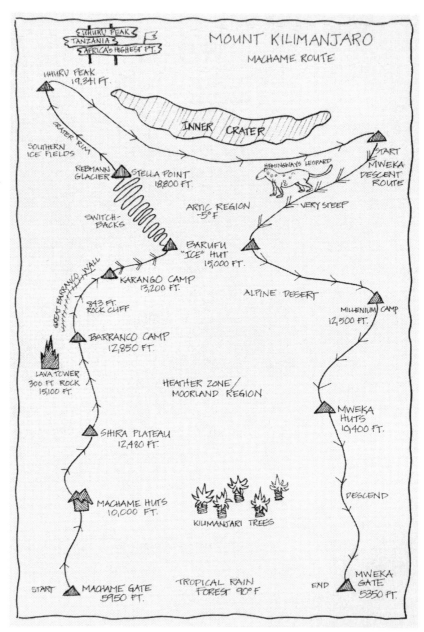

Mount Kilimanjaro Machame ascent route and Mweka descent.

Introduction

Kilimanjaro is a snow covered mountain 19,710 feet high, and is said to be the highest mountain in Africa. Its western summit is called Masai (*the House of God*). *Close to the western summit there is a dried and frozen carcass of a leopard. No one has explained what the leopard was seeking at that altitude.*

ERNEST HEMINGWAY, "THE SNOWS OF
KILIMANJARO"

––––––––––––––

Like the leopard, I am searching for something.

~ J.S.

1

Questing

THEY NEVER THOUGHT I'd really do it, so my wife and our daughters played along with my sudden obsession with climbing Mount Kilimanjaro. They assumed, wrongly it turned out, that in the face of their quiet acquiescence I'd train hard to climb the mountain, but I'd lose momentum when logistics got too complicated. When that happened, they hoped, I'd settle for a safer and less exotic goal. But as my training intensified month after month, my family recognized that nothing would stop me from traveling to Africa to attempt scaling Hemingway's great mountain. Seeing how meticulously I prepared physically and mentally, Carol, my wife, finally relented, with two stipulations. The first was that I had to promise to climb only as high as I could go safely, even if that meant quitting without reaching the summit. The second, her most emotional plea, was that I wouldn't do anything to risk my life. I made both promises freely, confident I'd have no trouble keeping them.

My confidence was misplaced. In the end, I broke both promises.

IT'S JUST BEFORE sunrise on August 13, 2011. We've been climbing since midnight. On our sixth day of climbing we're making the final push to the top of the crater rim of Mount Kilimanjaro in Tanzania. Even though we're near the Equator, it's brutally cold – so cold that my canteens are frozen solid and I can't feel my fingers. Thankfully, the night is almost over.

The full moon and millions of stars seem to follow us as we climb deliberately in single file behind our guide, Tobias. As the hours crawl I try to zone out. Plant pole. Breathe. Take a step. Repeat. The torch beam of my headlamp focuses on the boots of the climber just ahead of me, Sarah. Overhead I see the Rebmann Glacier, the colossal, silver, overhanging piece of ancient ice cap that crowns the square top of Kilimanjaro. Beyond that, to the east, is the rim of the massive volcano – closer now, but still beyond reach. Every crunching step we take sends loose bits of shale spilling down the slope under our feet. With a misstep, I could tumble in the same direction. The temperature dips below minus 20 Celsius. A chill creeps through each layer of my clothing, goading the blood in my extremities to freeze. With the incline now a steep thirty degrees, I plant my pole. Breathe. Take a step. Repeat.

Almost forgetting why I came here, more than once I've contemplated giving up. Each time, I recall what it took to get to Africa, thinking back to three years earlier when a pair of vicious illnesses ganged up on me; I swore that when I recovered I'd do something bold, to prove that I was still alive. And with the certainty I imagine Hemingway's leopard must have felt in venturing to such heights, I remember why I have to persevere.

Jay Scheiner

IN 2008, AT age forty-nine, I stared down prostate cancer and a heart condition. The cancer, detected after an unrelated urological surgery, was first just monitored by my urologists using an approach known as active surveillance. This consisted of blood tests, MRI's, and biopsies every few months to watch the cancer while it was still molecular. This passive approach dragged on for the better part of a year, completely contradicting the proactive way I normally manage life's details. What was I waiting for? To lose my best chance at a full cure while the cancer could possibly spread? Prostate cancer is rare in men below fifty. Because mortality statistics indicate that it's often more aggressive when diagnosed at a younger age, I couldn't understand why some doctors were recommending a delay in curative treatment.

The lack of closure became increasingly unacceptable to me, and caused lingering stress for my family, so I finally took charge of my care. After exploring all the options and gathering no fewer than *eight* second opinions, I put my full trust in the hands of a skilled surgeon, choosing to treat the cancer aggressively with radical prostatectomy: careful and complete surgical removal of the prostate followed by painful recovery and months of healing. The surgery proved successful; the cancer was gone.

During my recovery – and totally unrelated to the cancer – I developed atrial fibrillation, a dangerous, rapid and irregular heartbeat also known as supraventricular tachycardia, which landed me in the hospital again. The condition was initially diagnosed when my heart rate suddenly became erratic and approached 200 beats per minute. If untreated, a-fib can lead to a stroke. Most a-fib patients try to control the arrhythmias with medications that slow the heart rate, and blood thinners, but the drugs left me listless and once again searching for alternatives.

I imagined how it would have been if I hadn't been proactive with the prostate cancer months earlier: I'd still be dealing with invasive testing and uncertainty. To have to cope with both conditions simultaneously would have been intolerable; so I went with my gut once again and searched for a cure as opposed to containment.

We opted for the most aggressive treatment for a-fib: a five-and-a-half-hour surgical procedure called pulmonary vein isolation and ablation. My heart was stopped, and restarted several times with paddles, as electrophysiology cardiologists threaded catheters from one chamber of my heart to another to map, locate and cauterize the sections that were misfiring. During the three-month healing process, as the doctors weaned me off the blood thinners, I didn't know if the procedure had been successful. But thankfully, the operation worked – the arrhythmia was eliminated.

I could have been an incapacitated old man before the age of fifty. Instead, I was free to move forward.

Jay Scheiner

While determined to resume living, I couldn't quite shake the nagging fear that I wasn't really over the health crises, but only between them. A cloud trailed me – I couldn't seem to break out of my funk. Added to the year of coping with the illnesses, business pressures from the 2008 financial crisis aggravated the insomnia I'd struggled with for most of my adult life. While I'd always found my career rewarding and invigorating – I help families and businesses plan for the untimely death or disability of a loved one or business partner – now I began to make up excuses to avoid the office. There must have been a clinical name for what I was feeling, but I chose not to seek out professional help. Instead, I hunkered down to try to get through it on my own. Carol worried that if things continued on this trajectory I wouldn't want to work at all anymore. Clearly, I'd lost the spring in my step; 2009 and 2010 crept by in slow motion.

I knew full well I needed to change *something,* and sensed redemption would somehow come from a significant physical challenge. Find it. Train for it. Do it. Be me – the me I always tried to be. Be alive. And I needed to start *now* – before the window of opportunity closed forever – before another crisis; before a possible cancer recurrence; before the arrhythmia, a hereditary condition, developed in another part of my heart; before I got too damn old. I wanted and needed a way to test myself, an adventure – something meaningful – while I still had the chance. It had to be big; it had to be bold; it had to be an all-encompassing campaign, one I could become completely obsessed with and live for while still maintaining a reasonable work and family life.

Searching for my own personal crusade, I eliminated goals I couldn't realistically pursue. Before marrying Carol and starting our family, I made an eight-hundred-mile solo voyage from Port Washington, New York to Portland, Maine and back, in a nine-teen-foot sailboat. I'd hoped to set sail on my own once again, maybe to Bermuda or across the Atlantic, but taking such a huge risk now was out of the question. It was as untenable as swim-ming the English Channel, a challenge I considered in my youth but also dismissed as an adult. As an experienced long-distance cyclist, I'd thought about bicycling across the United States, but I couldn't spare eight weeks to ride thirty-five hundred miles from coast to coast. That same issue of time – I had to go to work after all – nixed hiking the Appalachian Trail, which would take half a year. The dream of a dream adventure persisted – I'd know it when I found it. I knew that I had two requirements for my adventure. After sufficient training and preparation, it had to be something I could complete in less than a month away from my business and family. And, there had to be a strong likelihood that I would survive the endeavor.

The idea of climbing Kilimanjaro hit me at my three-year post-cancer-surgery check-up. By then my business had recovered from the financial crisis so I had latitude to pursue an epic adventure. My surgeon, Dr. Ash Tewari, mesmerized me with the story of his own trek up Hemingway's mountain. Listening to him I recognized that a regular guy, in a profession that had nothing to do with extreme sports, could do something I'd always assumed could be done only by experienced mountaineers.

Maybe I could do it too. Climbing this mountain had never occurred to me, not in my wildest dreams – but now it *became* my wildest dream. The seed was planted, and the idea of climbing Mount Kilimanjaro started to become an obsession.

2

Training

I NEARLY BLEW up Amazon scooping up everything that could teach me anything about climbing Kilimanjaro: videos, guidebooks, memoirs, and maps. I attended seminars and grilled experts. Taking up hiking, then trekking, hooked and focused on the goal, I convinced myself that *I could be a mountain climber*, fear of heights be damned. Once the decision was made, and knowing that I had, at most, eight months to prepare before climbing season ended for the year, I had no intention of turning back.

Intensive training followed, beginning with daily two-hour workouts that soon turned into three-hour workouts; thousands of flights of stairs climbed; long city blocks walked and timed; hills run; and trainers obeyed. I walked to and from work. I walked to and from restaurants, whether two miles or six, at nine p.m. or midnight, in all kinds of weather. Once or twice a friend or two accompanied me on my post-restaurant hike.

Our friends thought what I was trying to do was a little cool, a little eccentric and extremely overambitious. Although they were too polite to say it, some of them viewed me as Don Quixote jousting with a windmill that masqueraded as a mountain.

Training hike on the Appalachian Trail, April, 2011 – four months
prior to traveling to Africa to climb Mount Kilimanjaro.

On weekends I hiked parts of the Appalachian Trail, mountains
along the Hudson River Valley, and the Catskills. On mountains with names like Storm King, Breakneck Ridge, and Mount
Defiance, I learned to scramble up rock, scale modest cliffs, and
put my lifelong aversion to heights in its place. I learned to treat
blisters and contend with hiking in sub-freezing temperatures. I
became reacquainted with skills thought lost, but only dormant,
in the decades since I was a sixteen-year-old Boy Scout. Best of
all, the spring in my step was back.

Training ferociously, I followed an aggressive daily, weekly and
monthly schedule, pushing myself harder and more faithfully than

ever in my life. Knowing that fewer than half of the climbers who attempt to reach Mount Kilimanjaro's 19,341-foot summit actually make it, in every conceivable way I tried to sway the odds in my favor.

While the financial commitment of climbing Mount Kilimanjaro was significant, the difference between a bare-bones approach and a safer but costlier option was worth it. After careful research, I chose a trekking company with operations based near Kilimanjaro – one of the most respected in the business – that appeared to offer the highest level of safety. Their staff-to-climber ratio was six to one. Their guides were certified high-altitude first responders, trained in basic battlefield first aid, including CPR, tourniquets, and treatment for blunt trauma. Every night the staff checked each climber's heart-rate and blood oxygen saturation. They had procedures in place to keep climbers alive during an evacuation. They had a chief medical officer on call. Equipment and tents were state-of-the-art, water purification methods were as safe as possible, and the food and cooking equipment more hygienic than other companies offered. The more I researched, the more this trekking company stood out.

As an insurance professional, I considered the added cost of doing it right as my premium for a safer climb, which would by extension increase the likelihood of my reaching the summit. I took every step to prepare for every contingency, even retaining Global Rescue, one of the world's leading international medevac companies, to provide emergency airlift to the United States if required. Carol was completely on board with spending whatever it took to bring me home safely.

Consulting with a nutritionist, I turned fat into muscle, dropped significant weight, and stepped up the karate training I'd been doing for many years. I researched and obsessed over clothing and equipment, including carbon fiber trekking poles, leather-and-Gore-Tex boots with custom insoles, high-intensity headlamp, woolen undergarments from New Zealand, backpack from Germany, and gloves fit to wear in Antarctica. An infectious disease doctor poked me repeatedly, immunizing me against yellow fever, typhoid, hepatitis, malaria, tetanus and meningitis. She gave me medications to carry with me, including Diamox, a prescription to take daily before and during the climb to help me acclimatize; Cipro, a potent antibiotic; and Decadron, a powerful steroid to be used as a last resort in case of severe headaches resulting from mountain sickness. My cardiologist jacked the treadmill up to *Everest Mode* before grudgingly sanctioning my climb. I worked to suppress my insomnia and gave up all sleeping aids, certain that I'd be so exhausted after each day on Kilimanjaro that I'd have no trouble falling asleep.

By the time I landed in Tanzania, stronger than I'd been in twenty years, it seemed as if my entire life had led up to this singular moment.

Still – what a selfish gamble! So much at risk. I wasn't *absolutely sure* I was up to this physical and mental challenge. At this stage of my life, should I have settled on a less dangerous way to prove myself to myself? Had I missed the chance to do something like this ten years ago when I was younger and stronger?

To complicate matters, I had information that I chose not to share with my family. I played down risks, fudged statistics, and minimized stories of incidents I'd come across while researching the climb. I didn't speak about climbers killed by falling rocks. I didn't mention reading about four deaths on Kilimanjaro in one week of 2007, including three porters who succumbed to hypothermia, and a trekker who died in her sleep from the effects of altitude sickness. During one of my dozens of training hikes, when I told a fellow climber I was preparing to climb Kilimanjaro, she tearfully confided that her cousin died on that mountain. *Don't do this*, she begged. *He thought he'd be fine and he wasn't.*

Jeannette Johnston, a Boston-based writer, told the most jarring story in an interview. On their final push to the summit, her team came across a man standing over his wife, who lay flat on the ground next to him; her lips were blue, and her chest was still. The couple had been on their way down from the summit with a porter when the wife collapsed; she died within minutes. Her name was Jennifer Mencken. She was 53, a rugged sportswoman and veteran mountain climber. She and her husband were on their belated honeymoon.

I didn't tell Carol these stories – and I didn't tell her that my route up Kilimanjaro would require me to scale at least one 800-foot cliff – concealing information that would have made her change her mind immediately. I suspected that, if she knew more about the risks, or even if she just developed a *feeling* of apprehension, she'd try to keep me from going and then I'd have to start over looking for a new quest. She let me plan to go fight my windmill, because she knew I was at my happiest when I could focus on a mission, yet she hoped and believed that ultimately I wouldn't follow through.

I hoped otherwise. Believing that *I* could overcome extreme temperatures and altitude sickness by pure strength of will, I rationalized that I could maybe... *bend...* my first promise to her. About the second promise – as my own best client I reasoned that if something terrible happened on that mountain at least my family would be protected financially, as I'd invested wisely and acquired a substantial amount of life insurance over the years. But if I had misjudged my readiness, or got caught in an avalanche or a rock slide, or if my arrhythmia returned at an extreme altitude – what an idiot! – I would leave behind three beautiful daughters, grown but not yet on their own, and a loving wife. No financial supplement could make up for the emotional damage I'd cause my family.

Saying our goodbyes at JFK International Airport wasn't easy. We'd been married for twenty-five years. The last thing Carol said to me was, *Come back to me, Jay.* I promised her I would.

3

Ascending

ON THE SIXTH night on the mountain, we continue to move in silence. Our climbing party includes Wendy, a commercial airline pilot and former Air Force captain, and Sarah, an attorney. Wendy and Sarah, both very cheerful and upbeat, create positive energy and a sense of optimism for our group. Larry, the fourth member of our team, is an American defense contractor living in Nigeria. Quiet, introspective and a little hard to read, Larry is a capable and disciplined climber; he freely shares his abundant knowledge of

From left – head guide Tobias, Sarah, Larry, Wendy & assistant guide Goudance. I am behind the camera.

Kilimanjaro and East Africa to help us understand more than we see. We're led by our chief guide, Tobias, who is about my height and muscularly trim; he's probably about ten years younger than me, with sad eyes and the bearing of a military commander. Tobias estimates he's climbed to the summit of Kilimanjaro around a hundred times. He's responsible for the safety of the entire group, including all of the porters; I sense that this responsibility weighs heavily on him. Goudance, our assistant guide, in his late thirties, is lighthearted and jovial. Taller than Tobias, Goudance is wiry and strong, with smooth skin that's black as night. When he smiles his joyful way brightens any mood. While Goudance is a licensed guide in his own right, it's clear that Tobias is the one in charge.

With (from left) head guide Tobias, rescue porter Isra and assistant guide Goudance in front of a giant senecio plant (Dendrosenecio kilimanjari, aka tree groundsel) in the alpine zone.

The Promise of Kilimanjaro

Mountaineering groups generally give themselves nicknames; for no good reason, we call ourselves Team Dirt. Trekking for five days straight, we've had to contend with an accelerated change of seasons, getting closer to the dead of an arctic winter by the hour. I've trained a lot to reach this point, but as the least experienced climber I'm having the hardest time at these extreme altitudes. Here, at 17,000 feet at three in the morning, it's brutally cold and I'm struggling to breathe. The most alarming theme for me, though, has been a near total lack of sleep.

THERE ARE SIX established routes to climb Kilimanjaro, and a dozen trekking companies leading expeditions. The trekking company I chose had a specific strategy to help us acclimatize over seven days. Their plan was classic Mountaineering 101: circle Kilimanjaro gradually instead of climbing straight up, and backtrack several thousand feet at the end of each day to sleep in denser air. Climbers making the more direct five-day ascent on the Marangu Route (sometimes called the Coca-Cola Route because climbers stay in huts that are more comfortable than tents, and porters bring along soft drinks to sell to the climbers) are much more likely to develop mountain sickness and fail to summit. On our seven-day Machame ascent route (often known as the Whiskey Route due to its reputation as a tougher physical climb) the summit success rate is higher because climbers have more time to adjust to the altitude.

The first day we rode by truck to Kilimanjaro National Park, past banana and coffee plantations. Tanzanian park authorities must know exactly who is on the mountain at all times; they want to make sure the proper fees are collected and that all climbers are accompanied by licensed local guides. Our guides coordinated check-in and registration at Machame Gate, the entrance to our route. There were dozens of climbing groups, people from all over the world, speaking languages I couldn't even identify, converging on this place to attempt climbing the world's tallest freestanding mountain. After check-in, we headed out.

Porters carrying heavy loads in the Heather Zone.

In Himalayan mountaineering, the local population that work at high altitude are called sherpas. In Africa they are called porters. Porters bear the heavy burdens of the trek; the most elite may eventually train to become guides. With twenty-four porters, cooks and runners assisting our two guides, we'd be self-sufficient for seven days.

We looked like a traveling circus. One porter carried three hundred eggs on his head. Another carried a giant sack of rice, also balanced precariously on his head, steadied by just the pinky of his left hand. One was wrapped in a tent with four folding chairs hanging from his belt loops. Another always winked at me, knowing he was the one responsible for my thirty-pound duffle bag. To them, this part of the journey through the forest was routine, as they'd climb the lower mountain whenever they could find an expedition to join. Fully acclimated to the altitude themselves because of their frequent climbs, the porters warned *pole, pole* (Swahili for slowly, slowly) urging us to take our time in hopes of dodging altitude sickness. By mid-afternoon all of our porters, toiling just for the benefit of four American climbers, had passed us on the trail.

Starting up the first 50 feet of the 834-foot cliff called The Great Barranco Wall on the morning of the fourth day. Our group resembled a traveling circus.

The Promise of Kilimanjaro

Kilimanjaro is home to four distinct climate zones: rainforest, low alpine, high alpine and glacial. Humidity is high and light mist or drizzle is common. Various flora such as orchids, ferns, fig and olive trees line the paths. The pure beauty of the environment made me feel like I'd discovered an enchanted forest. Giant ferns and mossy green trees, dripping with rainwater, painted the landscape. Hansel and Gretel would have found this setting familiar.

A week later, when I passed through these woods again on the way back down, I realized that I hadn't appreciated this spot's stunning beauty when I saw it the first time. The contrast between the lower mountain's rainforest, and the arctic climate above Kilimanjaro's crater rim, was jarring. On the way up, I couldn't appreciate the beauty or the grandeur. My mission was simple. Get to the top. Then get back down safely.

The narrow path led uphill through this little-acknowledged wonder of the world, over thousands of steps made from tree branches. Wendy and Sarah saw a monkey. I didn't. As we gained altitude the trail got ruttier and harder to navigate, but my training paid off as I easily kept pace with the guides and the other climbers. The scenery began to look more like a rugged forest and less like a jungle, bringing to mind Mount Defiance, one of my training sites in the Ramapo Mountains of New Jersey.

Machame Hut village marker, altitude approximately
10,000 feet, Night One. We climbed 4000 feet from
the base at Machame Gate, altitude 5950 feet.

Six hours after starting out we arrived at Machame Hut and
set up for our first night on Kilimanjaro. At an altitude of just
under 10,000 feet, we were now higher than Australia's highest
peaks; higher than Mount Washington, the tallest mountain
in the eastern United States; and more than twice as high as
I'd ever climbed in training. Our porters put up tents in the
forest, lit fires, and prepared the first of many hot meals on
the trail.

Both exhilarated and exhausted after ascending more than 4,000
feet on the first day, I assumed I'd nod off immediately. But I

couldn't sleep at all. I spent the entire night reading the trek-king guide over and over by the light of a mini-LED flashlight hanging from the top of my tent. By morning, at least I had the guidebook memorized. Facing a daylong trek on no sleep, with little reserve to call on, I convinced myself that I could keep going through pure will.

Emerging from the rainforest above 10,000 feet on the morning of the second day on the way to the Shira Plateau. From left - Tobias, Sarah, me and Larry.

Jay Scheiner

On the morning of the second day we left behind the last glades of the rainforest. Twenty miles away, our ultimate goal revealed itself to us – in Hemingway's words: *as wide as all the world, great, high, and unbelievably white in the sun, was the square top of Kilimanjaro.* The scenery was breathtaking. As we climbed, the humidity dropped and the lush jungle vegetation gradually gave way to grassy meadows and flowing fields of heather, protea, senecia, and giant lobelia. The path wound past an overhanging cave, past rocks and boulders, through a jagged ridge formed by an ancient lava flow. By early afternoon we glimpsed the edge of the Shira Plateau in the distance. The trail steepened, winding through thinning trees, as we continued uphill at a measured pace to help us acclimate to higher altitude; by this point we were starting to feel its effects. Everyone on our team felt some degree of nausea or headaches, which we knew was to be expected at this altitude. Staying hydrated would help combat its effects, so Team Dirt's unofficial soft drink became boiled stream water by the liter. Near sunset we reached Shira Camp at 12,480 feet. Climbing above this altitude, we'd be higher than any rescue helicopter in East Africa could fly to reach us.

In my tent I tried to record my impressions of the trek, but because I'd been awake for forty hours, my hands shook and I couldn't hold a pen. Out of desperation I made a tactical decision to take Benadryl to try to force myself to sleep, although we'd been warned not to use any sleep medication on the hike because the effects of altitude could cause a dangerous synergistic interaction. Conveniently forgetting – or ignoring – one of my promises, I took two little pink pills and awoke groggy in the morning after no more than five hours of sleep. Those five hours would be the last sleep I would have for the next four days, and I was already struggling with a 40-hour sleep deficit.

Nearing Lava Tower on the third day at an
altitude of approximately 15,000 feet.

ON THE THIRD day on Mount Kilimanjaro we hiked all morning toward Lava Tower, a looming, three-hundred-foot high volcanic mass attempted only by people with rock-climbing skills or a death wish. At the foot of the tower, 15,100 feet above sea level, we stopped for lunch. This was the highest I'd ever been in my life outside of an airplane. Nausea from the altitude slammed me, and I barely managed not to throw up. After lunch we descended 2,250 feet to Barranco, a spectacular campsite on the banks of a mountain stream at the foot of Kibo Peak, which loomed high above us. That night, struggling to take a deep breath, I prayed for sleep that never came, while worrying that even if I did fall asleep, I might not actually wake up.

By the next morning I'd been continuously without sleep for twenty-four hours since my attempt with Benadryl, which at sea level would have had the same effect as a blood-alcohol content of 0.10 percent. In all fifty states I would have been the equivalent of legally drunk; my judgment, attention, reaction time, hearing, memory, hand-eye coordination and decision-making were all compromised.

What if I never managed to sleep on this mountain? In this condition, could I actually have a chance of summiting Kilimanjaro? Could I continue to hide my insomnia from my guides and climbing partners? I'd have to, or Tobias would send me back down. I vowed to, and actually did, keep up with my companions. *Sleep on the mountain is overrated*, I convinced myself. *It's mind over matter.* Now was the time to call on the skills that had been ingrained in me since basic training.

After high school, I thought about joining the Coast Guard. At twenty, I considered leaving college to enlist in the Israeli Army. After law school, I was still searching for something. At twenty-five years old, I entered basic training to qualify as a special agent with the United States Drug Enforcement Administration (the DEA).

The training facility was located downwind from a giant paper mill in Glynco, Georgia. A former naval air base, Glynco housed a random collection of law enforcement agencies training their recruits. Some, such as our sister agencies in Customs, U.S. Marshals, and Secret Service, had missions similar to DEA. Others were secret units from foreign countries: small men in green fatigues we passed at the firing range and ran with on the obstacle course. We were forbidden to talk to them or about them for fear of compromising national security. In whispers, we learned they were called *Contras* - soldiers or guerrillas from Central America training to fight the communist Sandinistas of Nicaragua.

Our trainers, some of the finest law enforcement professionals in the world, rode us hard. Firearms and hand-to-hand combat instructors impressed upon us their philosophy of winning: *If you get shot, or stabbed, you'll probably live if you stay cool and have a winning attitude. Trust your team to neutralize the threat and the medical professionals to save you. If you give up, if you lack the courage to fight on, you'll die.*

For twelve weeks we were challenged, and those of us who made it to graduation and survived our probationary year as Special

Agents of the DEA, had the confidence of knowing we'd been prepared for success at all costs.

DEA graduation day at Federal Law Enforcement Training Center with friends Robert Joice (center) and Javier Peña (left). Bob went on to become a Ph.D./economist. Javier had a storied career in DEA, spending years in Colombia tracking Pablo Escobar, founder of the Medellin drug cartel, to successful conclusion in 1993. Javier's role in the manhunt for Escobar was featured in the Netflix series "Narcos."

Sleep on the mountain is overrated, I convinced myself. *If I have to, I'll deal with it and go on.*

Climbing up a steep section of rock just ahead
of assistant guide Goudance.

The fourth day began with scaling the jagged, near-vertical rock
face of the Great Barranco Wall. The trick was to move deliberately
with each step and use all four limbs to scramble up the 843-foot
cliff. The guides chanted *pole, pole*. The Barranco Wall was one of
the most treacherous parts of the climb. It would test my training,
and my commitment to conquer my fear of heights. Though I'd
trained for it rigorously, the Barranco Wall was even more massive
than I'd anticipated. The half-year of disciplined work brought com-
petence in climbing with my hands, legs, body and mind. I almost
burst with pride when I looked down, about 1,000 feet beyond the
edge of the giant cliff, nearly fearless. Being alive to appreciate this
adventure had brought immeasurable joy; not only was I scaling
this mountain: I felt I had become one with the mountain.

At that moment, in that place, I recalled a line from T. E. Lawrence – Lawrence of Arabia – that summed up everything I wanted to accomplish through this endeavor: *Those who dream by night in the dusty recesses of their minds wake in the day to find that it was all vanity; but the dreamers of the day are dangerous men, for they may act their dream with open eyes, and make it possible.* Hanging from the side of this giant cliff in the heavy morning fog, scaling East Africa's Great Barranco Wall, I felt closer than I'd ever been – or ever would be again – to being the *dreamer of the day.*

Making our way up a slippery section of rock at an altitude of approximately 14,000 feet on day four. From left, Wendy, Sarah, Larry, me, and rescue porter Isra.

Once we scrambled over the final boulders and edged our way over the cliff, the fog began to lift, and I looked down to savor our accomplishment. From now on, the terrain would be more moderate as we descended into the Karanga Valley.

Before nightfall of the fourth day we made camp. High altitude sucks muscle from your body, and we required massive amounts of food to compensate. Even though I probably took in four thousand calories a day, I knew my weight was dropping. The porters prepared thick African stew and rice, which I couldn't get enough of.

Porters and cooks preparing our campsite at Karanga Camp at an elevation of 13,200 feet. We arrived late in the afternoon of the fourth day after descending several thousand feet to help us acclimate to the altitude.

Jay Scheiner

During the nightly medical-status check by our head guide, Tobias, I intentionally neglected to mention my persistent lack of sleep. I'd failed to mention it every day since beginning our ascent, out of concern that Tobias might make me turn back if he knew. Sleeplessness was my personal demon; unable to sleep at altitude, I found the nights endless, and thought I might go insane. Every night, as soon as I settled into my tent, my mind would begin racing like a Ferrari and wouldn't shut down as I obsessed over every detail of what had already happened and what was in store. Each night began with arranging and rearranging my muddy boots and all of my gear inside a cramped tent so everything would be relatively dry in the morning. As I lay awake, nursing a cough that never went away, I'd play and replay in my mind how I was going to fit everything back into the pack the next day. I couldn't help but catastrophize.

Every time I drifted to the edge of sleep, I'd gasp for air and jolt awake. At such extreme altitudes even taking in air had to be a conscious, purposeful act; I became convinced that if I fell asleep I'd stop breathing and die. Don Quixote, delusional from staying awake to pursue his obsessions, came to mind.

No one can function in extreme altitude day after day without sleep. All logic should have led me back down the mountain, but in the middle of the night I perseverated about how I'd have to explain, for the rest of my life, why I'd abandoned my climb halfway up Kilimanjaro. If I gave up, I'd have failed myself – and everything

I did to get to Africa would have been for nothing. Freezing in my tent and half-crazy from lack of sleep, I was overwhelmed worrying about the opinions of people eight thousand miles away.

What people thought shouldn't have mattered to me. Those close to me would have understood; if they'd seen how compromised I was, they would have insisted I come down immediately. Determination to prove that I could succeed pushed me to continue, risks be damned, to the point where I lost sight of my promises and my senses.

Meanwhile, as I fixated on everything that could go wrong, my companions appeared to drift off into snoring sleep in the tents around me, serene as Sancho Panza, Quixote's squire: *All I know is that while I'm asleep, I'm never afraid, and I have no hopes, no struggles, no glories – and bless the man who invented sleep, a cloak over all human thought.* The less I slept, the more I craved it. I would have given anything to be able to sleep.

By the morning of the fifth day I'd been sleepless for forty-eight hours straight. After forty-eight hours of sleeplessness the body begins shutting down for microsleeps, episodes similar to blackouts, that last less than a minute. Reaction times are shot. Occasionally when we stopped on the trail, I managed to nod off for a moment by leaning on my trekking poles and turning myself into a tripod. The few seconds of near-sleep I snagged felt like a tease, though; I was more than a little jealous of anyone actually getting consecutive hours of the real thing.

Despite my sleeplessness, the beauty and alienness of the experience were overwhelming. The scenery in the high alpine desert looked more like the moon than planet Earth. Lava formations from eruptions 360,000 years ago left rocky ruins reminiscent of Stonehenge or a maze. But these were not made by men. During the days of climbing above the clouds, staying in tiny tents in primitive conditions near the top of a cold, gigantic mountain, surrounded by spectacular scenery and the sounds of Swahili, I felt that, sleep or no sleep, I wouldn't want to be anywhere else.

Lava formations, unchanged for thousands of years, form a natural maze.

Stopping to rest in the high alpine desert on day five.

We climbed out of the thin air of the Karanga Valley at the start of the fifth day, heading east and then north for several hours, through the bleak high alpine desert. Our target was the strategically-placed rocky perch called Barafu Hut, where the temperature was barely above freezing when we arrived in mid-afternoon. At the aptly-named Barafu – *ice* in Swahili – we could see glaciers high above us to the northwest. Walking repeatedly up and down thirty flights of stairs in our apartment building in New York City had prepared me for trials like this. After hours of climbing, we scrambled up rock to the top of the Barafu ridge, where Uhuru Peak, Kilimanjaro's glorious summit, came into full view, even more dramatic than I'd anticipated. At an altitude of 15,000 feet, we were now higher than the Matterhorn, and well above the height of Mount Rainier, the highest glacial peak in the continental United States.

During the day, solar radiation was high. Now, with the sun going down, the temperature would plummet to well below freezing. We'd find no fresh drinking water here; all potable water has to be dragged up from 13,000 feet. This was the last stop before our final ascent toward Uhuru Peak. Twenty-two porters and cooks who'd looked after us over the past four days would climb no higher; our traveling circus would be pared down to a handful of performers, as only two highly-skilled guides and two rescue porters would accompany us to the roof of Africa. The rest of the team would wait at Barafu Hut until our return from the summit twelve to fourteen hours later.

Insomnia continued to take its toll: I felt like a snail trying to keep up with a herd of goats. Even wearing summit goggles during the daytime to repel ninety percent of the light, I was beginning to have trouble with my eyesight. By the last night of the ascent I knew I should admit to my climbing partners and guides that I hadn't slept in three nights and make the intelligent choice to quit. I was part of a team; we were all dependent on each other. I had a choice to remain at Barafu or continue toward the summit; by continuing, I could place the rest of our team at risk, as I was clearly the weakest link. At this pivotal moment, in every conceivable way, I never should have climbed higher. But the combination of altitude, insomnia, and misplaced ambition skewed my rational thought. I was about to risk breaking my most important promise: the one about not endangering my life.

View of Kibo, Kilimanjaro's highest summit, from Barafu (*Ice*)
Hut at the end of the fifth day at altitude 15,000 feet. Barafu sits
on a narrow ledge surrounded on one side by a high grouping
of rocks (foreground) and a sheer cliff on the other side.

During our last meal before starting out on the all-night summit
attempt, I admitted to my companions that I'd be willing to lose
a toe or a finger or a few of each in exchange for making it to the
top of Mount Kilimanjaro. I could tell they thought I was being
overdramatic. I didn't let on that I was completely serious.

Jay Scheiner

WE BEGIN THIS sixth day on Kilimanjaro, when we'll finally push for the summit, at midnight, each wearing every piece of clothing we have. I have multiple layers on top and bottom, including hats, a face mask, and three pairs of socks under my mountaineering boots. Of course, I'm wearing my South Pole gloves. Within reach, stuffed in many pockets and mixed in with the layers of clothing, are all the other things I might lose track of while dealing with too many pockets or not enough oxygen, including headlamp, power bars, medical kit, and vital prescription medications in case conditions deteriorate up above. By now I've been sleep-deprived for sixty-six hours. Always on the lookout for Hemingway's leopard – even though I know it mysteriously disappeared from its resting place sometime in the 1930s – I scour the landscape for a glimpse, or a hint of its spirit.

Fine glacial silt covers the slopes above us that reach up to ring Kilimanjaro's summit, with the southern ice fields and the Rebmann Glacier visible even here below Kilimanjaro's crater rim. Each guide carries nearly seventy pounds of gear, including safety equipment, large oxygen tanks, and masks for each climber. Isra, our primary rescue porter, carries a portable hyperbaric chamber called a Gamow bag, a folding stretcher, and half an emergency room in his eighty-five-pound pack. I carry no such heavy burdens; I'm responsible only for lugging *myself* the last several thousand feet to the top of the mountain.

At an altitude of 17,000 feet, as we enter the glacial zone and near arctic conditions, I'm having serious trouble. To an outsider it would probably look as if a zombie were trailing our small climbing party, stumbling with each labored step and mumbling almost incoherently. I'd see him if I looked in a mirror, for he is me.

My journey to Kilimanjaro involved twenty-four hours of travel, with layovers in Amsterdam and Dar es Salaam. After more than a day spent traveling, carrying all the equipment I'd need for the climb, I arrived at a small airport near Moshi, a city near the mountain. Here, I met up with my guides and climbing partners. We spent several days learning equipment and procedures, and preparing to set out for the mountain.

Tanzania, about twice the size of California, is home to a wide range of climates and scores of spoken languages. The country is protective of its independence and history, and Kilimanjaro is the jewel in its crown, attracting thousands of adventure tourists every year. Although Tanzania is one of the poorest nations in the world, it is rich in natural resources, including gold, diamonds, uranium, and a blue-violet gemstone called Tanzanite. Tanzanite is mined exclusively in an eight-kilometer-square patch at the foot of Mount Kilimanjaro; it's found nowhere else in the world. According to a Tanzanian geologist, *the circumstances that led to its formation 585 million years ago were so exceptional that the likelihood of finding Tanzanite anywhere else on earth is one in a million, making it a thousand times rarer than diamonds.* Although its coloring is similar to a blue sapphire, Tanzanite is much more fragile.

While staying in Moshi before heading out to Kilimanjaro, I met with a gem dealer named Patience, the only honest jeweler in all of Tanzania (according to the trekking company). He helped me select a stunning, pear-shaped, deep-blue stone. I promised myself that on safe completion of the trek I'd bring it home for Carol. The beauty, fragility and rarity of Tanzanite, and its association with Kilimanjaro, seemed to carry a special connection with the climb and my promise to return home safely.

4

Struggling

BRITISH PHOTOJOURNALIST JOHN Reader described the final attempt at Kilimanjaro's summit as *the equivalent of clambering up the side of nine Empire State Buildings laid end to end at sixteen degrees.* The last push to the top of the mountain begins at 15,000 feet; here, the air is only half as dense as you'd find at sea level. The climber attempts those feats *with the equivalent of only one lung; the result is agonizing, there is no other word for it.*

Some have called Kilimanjaro *Everyman's Everest,* because it can be ascended without advanced equipment like ropes, crampons and ice axes, or advanced mountaineering skills. This doesn't mean, though, that the climb can be completed without careful physical and mental preparation. Climbing Kilimanjaro requires months of practice and conditioning. The atmosphere ranges from tropical to arctic. Sparse oxygen at higher altitudes causes extreme weakness and discomfort. Many parts of the mountain are steep and treacherous. More than half of those who begin suffer from altitude sickness and never make it to the peak, especially those who take shorter routes and ignore the need to acclimate to thinner air and climate extremes. Even a superbly fit climber can fail if he or she lacks the grit to make it all the way to the top.

The beauty of the upper mountain is stunning; the temperature
falls as we ascend. Here with chief guide Tobias and rescue porter
Isra, who carries the emergency supplies and Gamow Bag.

At this extreme altitude I'm finding plant and animal life scarce,
while human life is not; climbers are abundant. Nobody climbs
Kilimanjaro alone. Every climber is part of a team, and every week
during the climbing season dozens of teams tackle the mountain,
winding their way to the top or heading back down. Approaching
the top of the mountain, you may encounter bottlenecks of climbers heading the opposite direction, some so beaten by altitude sickness that they have to be dragged down by porters. In many ways
the scene resembles airport security on a holiday weekend; the
switchbacks – shallow, winding paths meant to lessen the angle of
the climb and slow the progress of climbers – bring to mind the

back-and-forth of an airport security line. But at least an airport offers a bearable climate and reasonable lighting. Imagine the temperature in the terminal diving from seventy degrees Fahrenheit to five degrees below zero. Tilt the floor to a twenty-degree slope and replace the smooth tile with marbles and chunks of broken slate. Keep an eye out for patches of vomit left by someone in line ahead of you, and add airborne dust whipped up by a strong, incessant wind. Then block one nostril to make it twice as hard to get sufficient oxygen. Finally, turn out all the lights. That's 3:00 am on Mount Kilimanjaro, on the way to the summit, at 17,000 feet above sea level.

Some ascent routes are known for frequent rock-falls. Our route avoided ascent of the more unstable sections, such as Kilimanjaro's Western Breach.

Even some world class athletes have failed to reach the summit. Tennis great Martina Navratilova had to be rescued off the mountain after suffering high-altitude pulmonary edema – fluid accumulation in the lungs. Of those mere mortals who attempt the climb each year, more than a thousand, most of them remarkably well-trained and fit, are evacuated; while around ten deaths are reported annually, very likely more go unreported for fear that adventure tourists will be scared away. Deaths also occur each year among the African porters and guides who carry the heaviest burdens and keep the climbers safe. From the beginning of any climb, as climbers aspire to ever higher altitudes, their bodies have to acclimate to decreasing oxygen pressure. Failure to acclimatize can cause acute mountain sickness (AMS) symptoms, including sleeplessness, lightheadedness, fatigue, headache, loss of appetite, nausea or vomiting, rapid pulse, and shortness of breath. AMS can quickly become extremely serious and, although rarely, fatal.

The Promise of Kilimanjaro

AFTER SIX HOURS of climbing through darkness, with the crowd finally thinning out, our Team Dirt continues. As we make slow progress, several summit parties pass us by on their way to the top; we meet others coming down after they've had to give up. We've reached the top of our sixth Empire State Building. We're being lashed by powerful winds that make the distance past the Rebmann Glacier toward Stella Point, the entry point at the top of the crater rim, seem insurmountable. I can't imagine continuing any longer. The positive thoughts that helped me put one foot in front of the other for so many hours fade as I waste energy just catching my breath. Still, the brightest stars I've ever seen pierce through the black night and seem to lead me on a path I'm compelled to follow.

We still have several hours and one Empire State Building left to climb. Having already asked the guides to stop for me several times, I refuse to make another request. Just put one foot in front of the other. Plant pole. Breathe. Cough. Take a step. Repeat. I'm concerned that I'll have to explain for the rest of my life why I didn't make it to the top of this mountain. Then again, there's this gnawing fear that the rest of my life might actually *play itself out* on this mountain.

My resting pulse rate rises well above one hundred beats per minute. The heartbeat seems regular, but what if my a-fib returns now, at these extreme altitudes? And then there's my secret: I haven't told anyone that I haven't slept since my ill-advised experiment with Benadryl nearly seventy-two hours ago. If the guides learn the extent of my insomnia, they'll surely end my climb and force me to descend the mountain.

Sun rising over Mawenzi, Kilimanjaro's eastern summit,
on the morning of the sixth day. The desolate area
between the two peaks is called the Saddle.

The sun makes its slow rise over Mawenzi, Kilimanjaro's eastern summit, which is rarely attempted; we're climbing Kibo – Kili's western, highest peak. The ground underfoot, the *scree*, is a combination of shale and gravel. Poor traction forces us to slip back half a step for every step forward as we dig our poles into the scree. The howling wind picks up and the topsoil of the slope becomes airborne as we forge on through the emerging light. I take out my goggles, but it's too late: gritty dust stings both of my eyes, temporarily blinding me. Other than the Barranco Wall, this is by far the steepest part we've encountered, yet my only fear involves not making it to the top. Fighting the backsliding makes it that much harder to advance.

I *must* get to the top of this mountain, which is so close now. It's 7:30 am. We've been climbing in the dark all night; the sun finally appeared an hour ago. Moving with extreme care we reach the volcano's tip and climb over the edge. I hug the wooden sign reading *YOU ARE NOW AT STELLA POINT ALT. 5730 AMSL* – meters above mean sea level, which is 18,800 feet, but to reach the true summit, five hundred feet higher and on the other side of the volcano's peak, we'll have to stagger westward around the rim of Kilimanjaro for more than an hour.

Immediately after crawling over the crater rim we're blasted by strong winds, so we take shelter behind a grouping of giant volcanic rocks. Aside from near total exhaustion, my most immediate concern now is that I can't see. Something's very wrong: I can barely open my eyes, which feel like they're about to pop out of my face. I confide to Sarah that I think I might be done; maybe I should wait at Stella Point until the group returns. She and Wendy urge me to finish the climb with them. Tobias isn't in on this discussion. If he learns that I'm thinking about not continuing

Perched high up on a rock – my trekking poles ever my companions.

he won't break established protocol to let me stay alone at Stella Point for two hours while the rest of the group treks to the summit and back. If I give up now Tobias will appoint Goudance, our assistant guide, to descend with me, leaving Sarah, Wendy and Larry with just one guide, and vulnerable if anything happens to them near the top. This I can't accept. I don't want to jeopardize their safety or their chance of summiting, so I agree to continue with them toward the peak. Team Dirt remains intact.

Once I decide to continue, I vow that nothing will stop me from getting to the top of Mount Kilimanjaro. In spite of my promise to my family, the idea of quitting before reaching the summit actually sickens me. When I was seventeen, I learned more than I wanted to know about failure and disappointment – and the lessons are never far from my heart. This is going to be my chance to put those lessons in their place – finally.

My decision not to give up carries near fatal consequences.

5

Crossing

THEY NEVER THOUGHT I'd really do it, so when I was seventeen my parents played along with my obsession with attempting to become the youngest person to sail solo across the Atlantic.

My father was an accomplished sailor, but my siblings never took to it the way I did. I was born to sail. My brother's hero was Mickey Mantle and my sister idolized George Harrison. *My* hero was Robin Lee Graham, a teenager who sailed west from Los Angeles to circle the world alone. Reading and rereading Robin's book, "Dove," I was captivated. He was brave. He was cool. He met a beautiful girl in Tahiti and fell in love. When he finished his round-the-world voyage Robin was twenty-one, while I was barely entering my teens, but I vowed that someday I'd sail away too, and maybe, just maybe, I'd become the youngest person ever to sail alone across the Atlantic.

A bit of a loner, I was content and focused on my dream. In a time before GPS I learned the dark arts of basic celestial navigation, seamanship, and Morse code. Offshore sailboat racing was the key to gaining experience, and at sixteen I was selected to join a racing crew, voyaging to Nova Scotia and Bermuda.

Jay Scheiner

My father, an inventor, had worked in the boating industry. He created rigging systems that made boats faster and safer, and received a patent for the first modern furling headstay, which allowed small crews to shorten sail in rough weather without venturing onto a slick foredeck. I would need his experience and help with planning and logistics. When push came to shove, though, my parents told me I could attempt to find sponsors but they declined to fund the endeavor, hoping I'd give up.

I wrote letters and made phone calls, soliciting dozens of manufacturers, outlining a detailed plan to generate publicity for them in exchange for equipment and a boat suitable for an ocean crossing. Ultimately, to my parents' dismay and my satisfaction, I persuaded Thomas Hale, owner of Martha's Vineyard Shipyard, to build a *Vineyard Vixen*, a seagoing 29-foot sloop, for me to use. I had the skills, the knowledge, the offshore sailing experience, the motivation – and now I had the means. By the time I was scheduled to set sail, at eighteen, I would be a year younger than Robin Lee Graham was when he soloed the Atlantic.

Before finalizing our arrangement, Mr. Hale asked to speak to my parents, to make sure they were on board with the plan. I thought it wouldn't be a problem, that my parents would live up to their assurance that I could go if I got a sponsorship. But my father took me aside when I got back from Martha's Vineyard, buoyant with the excitement of the sponsorship and the reality of the voyage. He sat me down and looked at me in a way I'd never seen before. *I know you're capable and it's what you want more than anything, Jay,* he said. *But there's a real chance that you'll get caught in a storm, or fall overboard, or get run down by a freighter. You don't know what can happen out in the Atlantic, no matter how prepared you are. Your mother and I couldn't survive if we lost you.*

I was devastated. I couldn't do it without my father's consent, or his experience in logistics and planning. I had no choice but to give up my quest. A few months later, Robert Gainer, an American boy my age, slipped silently into England's Falmouth Harbor on his *Sea Sprite* sloop. He sailed three thousand miles from Rhode Island, effectively fulfilling the dream that was mine. Gainer went on to become a renowned sailor and adventurer. I went on to college and law school.

In my disappointment, I couldn't fathom why my parents wouldn't let me pursue what I believed was my destiny. Even in adulthood I regarded my lost shot at crossing the Atlantic as a complete failure. All subsequent adventures, including a solo voyage to Maine when I was nineteen, were merely consolation prizes. I resolved never to quit anything I'd committed to ever again, and I stuck to that resolution. It wasn't until I became a parent myself that I understood that protecting your children, often from themselves, comes before anything else.

Now, on this mountain, I resolved to push on, regardless.

During 800-mile solo round trip voyage from Port Washington, New York to Portland, Maine in 1978. My consolation prize for passing on the chance to cross the Atlantic solo.

The southern ice fields, ancient glaciers, at approximately 19,000
feet on the way to the true summit at 8:00 am on the sixth day.

Jay Scheiner

ONCE WE EMERGE from the shelter of the giant rocks we begin the painfully slow, counter-clockwise slog around the rim toward the true summit. This route is more gradual than the steeply-pitched climb to the top of the volcano. We trek past the southern ice field and the snows of Kilimanjaro – Hemingway's snows – which are actually ten-thousand-year-old glaciers. They're not nearly as towering as I'd imagined, for they're on their own death march, melting – actually evaporating – until sometime in the not-too-distant future when they'll disappear forever. Eyes stinging and head clanging, by now I can barely make out the beauty of my surroundings. My eyeballs are being forced out of their sockets. If I were honest with myself, I'd have to admit that I'm showing clear signs of acute mountain sickness. I try to concentrate on a red string hanging from Tobias's backpack to stay on track; I might be grasping at it as I blindly follow him, but I'm not even sure. I remember the trekker's expression: *your altitude is determined by your attitude.* I'll continue on no matter what – at all costs – for I am one hundred percent committed now. Above the clouds the landscape looks extraterrestrial. Even in my addled state, I know it is heaven, and I am so very close to it.

On our way to the summit we pass trekkers who have begun
their descent and are making their way back around the
volcano to the point where they can descend steeply.

RISING MAJESTICALLY FROM the Tanzanian plains near Kenya, Mount Kilimanjaro can be seen from ninety-five miles away in every direction. Kilimanjaro is one of the world's largest volcanoes; even though it hasn't erupted in thousands of years, it's not technically extinct. It remains the highest free-standing mountain in the world. Other, higher mountains, like Everest, K2 and Annapurna, spring up from a *range* of mountains, so they aren't as tall from their base to their peak as Kilimanjaro. Mount Kilimanjaro was first documented when the geographer Ptolemy of Egypt recorded a great snow mountain in the 2nd century AD. In 1849, a German missionary named Rebmann reported seeing a snow-capped mountain but was ridiculed by the Royal Geographical Society, whose members scoffed at the idea of snow at the Equator. The first successful summit was forty years later by German geology professor and mountaineer Hans Meyer.

When Hemingway wrote "The Snows of Kilimanjaro," after visiting Africa in 1933, few people had climbed the mountain. The trek would have been more treacherous in Hemingway's time; back then the marked trails didn't exist and the glaciers presented a more formidable barrier to the summit. In fact, Hemingway himself never set foot on the mountain.

This is a view from the summit looking into Kilimanjaro's giant crater. The ice that has capped the mountain in permanent glacier for thousands of years is now a fraction of what it once was.

6

Summiting

WE CAN SEE it long before we reach it: a primitive, hand-carved wooden sign that proclaims *CONGRATULATIONS YOU ARE NOW AT UHURU PEAK TANZANIA 5895 MAMSL.* Breathless from excitement, exertion, and insufficient oxygen, we trudge around the rim of the massive volcano, passing climbers who reached the summit at sunrise and have already begun their descent.

We arrive at the sign, and the mountain's true summit, at 8:30 am. After climbing for more than eight hours in sub-zero temperatures through another sleepless night, I cannot believe I'm finally standing at the summit of Mount Kilimanjaro, the object of my obsession. Amazingly, even at 19,341 feet, surrounded by the purest, cleanest – and thinnest – air in Africa, the sign is plastered with graffiti and stickers advertising sportswear manufacturers and radio stations, even Nick's Famous Roast Beef Restaurant. All are slapped haphazardly on this sacred marker by people who have attained the summit of this geographical wonder, yet see nothing wrong with marring its sanctity.

We wait to be photographed at the most famous sign in Africa. A German group ahead of us takes pictures of every climber at every angle, positioning themselves as if they're posing for a wedding album. Finally it's our turn to monopolize the sign and scenery, and we do the same thing, shooting photos of each and all of us, alone, as a group, in pairs, with our guides, without our guides. All around us, as Sarah, Wendy and Larry tell me, is the view of a lifetime. If only I could see it clearly.

Team Dirt arrives at Mount Kilimanjaro's 19,341-foot summit at 8:30 am. From left - Goudance, Larry, Wendy, Sarah, me and Tobias.

When the photos are done we sit next to the sign, near the edge of the giant crater that houses the ancient Furtwangler glacier. I touch one of the sign's support pillars to my cheek and hold myself fast to it, barely believing I'm here. Even through my woolen balaclava I can feel how cold and rough the wood is. Wendy takes video of each of us. Larry sounds like a professor. I'm speaking absolute gibberish.

My solo summit portrait. I'm smiling for this photo, as my mother trained me to do. Here, standing at the highest point of Africa, is where my eyes and body and mind have already started to lose any sense of measured control.

Something is seriously wrong: I've stayed in the thin air, close to 20,000 feet, way too long. For me, there's no more air to breathe. My heart is racing and my sight is diminished. My head spins and I'm desperately thirsty, but my canteen is still frozen. I suspect I might not be thinking clearly when I consider puncturing my arm and sucking my own blood to quench my thirst. Now it occurs to me that I may not survive the descent of this mountain.

It's well past the time to trek back around the crater rim and head down the mountain, which apparently we do. I squint through swollen eyes to catch a glimpse of the grandeur of the southern ice fields, and imagine floating eastward down a crunching frozen hill, a mixture of dirt with the thinnest ice shield on top. My actual memory of this forty-minute interval is disjointed, though, like a hazy image from childhood that might be true, even though there's no solid proof that it actually happened.

At 9:30 am, just as we reach the edge of the precipice, where we can begin to descend steeply, I simply implode.

7

Freefalling

SOMEONE MUST BE whacking me repeatedly on the back of the head with a baseball bat. I sit down – or fall down – and stay there. Tobias measures my blood oxygen saturation. A normal reading would top ninety-five percent; any drastic drop in oxygen saturation is life-threatening. Organ damage can occur at less than eighty percent; less than sixty-five percent can lead to mental impairment; oxygen saturation below fifty-five percent can lead to loss of consciousness. My oxygen saturation level is fifty-eight percent.

I'm disoriented. Vulnerable. My heart is pounding. And, six thousand feet too high for a helicopter rescue, I'm absolutely terrified. I haven't slept in seventy-five hours. Goudance sets up an oxygen tank and hangs the plastic tubing around my neck. I gasp like a newborn taking its first breath. Even I can tell that I'm displaying early signs of high-altitude cerebral edema – swelling of the brain due to acute mountain sickness. The related symptom of bulging eyeballs earlier should have been a warning to cut short my climb. I take Decadron, a powerful steroid used to reduce swelling in the brain. Decadron is nearly the last resort in cases of altitude sickness, just short of having to be zipped into the pressurized Gamow bag and carried down the mountain on a stretcher. If you get to the point where you have to take Decadron, all bets are off: no matter where you are, you must immediately begin to descend the mountain.

Altitude 18,800 feet at 9:30 am after hiking back from the summit around the rim of the volcano. I'm seated at left, being treated with oxygen (note tubing) and Decadron prior to descending. At this point I'd been awake for 75 hours. Where the land meets the clouds in the background is the edge of the mountain. From here the mountain falls almost straight down. This was the quickest descent route.

After twenty minutes I'm stable enough to continue. I realize I'll either have to walk many hours down this steep mountain until the sun sets, or be rescued. Or I may also die on this mountain. It scares the living crap out of me. I've already broken my first promise, and now it appears I've broken the second. I ignored the desperate signals my body was trying to send me – messages from God, maybe? – insisting that I go home to my family. Hemingway said the only *real* sports are mountain climbing and bull fighting. What wouldn't I give to be back down at sea level right now – even facing a charging bull. I'd give anything. Everything.

The descent path for all climbers ascending Kilimanjaro on the Machame Route is called the Mweka Route. Mweka offers two options for beginning the descent from the edge of the crater rim. The slower option, easier on nerves and knees, begins by retracing the back-and-forth switchbacks of the night before. The straight path, on the other hand, calls for a wild and slippery descent across the ice field from Stella Point; this route is as severely pitched and hair-raising as a double black diamond run on a ski slope. Tobias has Goudance, and a summit porter carrying my backpack, launch me down the side of the volcano in a near free-fall; it's the fastest way down the mountain to safety. What's going through my fried brain as I plummet straight down? I honestly don't know. Later, all I recall is thinking *I have to get home. I have to get home. I have to get down this mountain under my own power, no matter what, and not have to be carried.* Goudance steadies me as we tumble straight down the outer face of the volcano, kicking dust, sand and crumbling rock into our own faces. A jolt of panicked adrenaline cancels out my hours of sleeplessness and keeps me focused.

By this time, charging well ahead of Tobias and the other members of our climbing group, we're not just descending – we're running and sliding straight down Kilimanjaro. Goudance's strategy seems to be getting me to a lower altitude as fast as possible, before my head explodes. With my eyes still bulging, my vision remains compromised. My trekking poles and many layers of clothing act as shock absorbers as I fall every so often.

We stop several times to replenish my oxygen. At this elevation, my saturation is at acceptable levels only while I'm hooked up to the tank, but the tank can't be used during hiking, let alone while tumbling 4,000 feet from the edge of a volcano at a thirty-degree slope. Each break gives me a few minutes to think about just how far I still have to go to reach a safe altitude. My attention skips through thoughts and memories so fast that I can't keep up, exactly the way my mind jumps from subject to subject as I lie awake at night. Will I have to be evacuated from this mountain? Is there anything left in me to continue?

High up in the clouds.

The Promise of Kilimanjaro

My brain is on fire as I lean against what looks like a giant moon rock and suck on the oxygen. I can't help berating myself for getting into this predicament; this is probably the dumbest thing I've ever done. I recall the smartest thing I ever did: not the college or career I selected, but choosing the right life partner. Carol *gets me,* and takes everything I throw at her with poise and good humor. Together, we've built a life, and I need to muster the will to keep going down this mountain so I can return to it, and never jeopardize it again.

As we continue to plummet down Kilimanjaro in barely-controlled free-fall, my mind races faster than my legs can run. I recall the truck ride six days ago to our starting point, the Machame Gate, with my climbing partners. We spoke about what the climb meant to us. I told Wendy and Sarah that this would be the grandest adventure of my lifetime; I'd never be able to attempt anything this monumental again. I'd never have another shot at a 20,000-foot high adventure in Africa, reaching nearly four miles up to the heavens. For me, this was the real deal, my one shot at a significant challenge. At thirty-something, full of optimism and free of ties, Sarah and Wendy couldn't understand my motivation. Wendy's already climbed Mont Blanc and Mount Rainier; now she's aiming at Aconcagua, South America's tallest peak. Sarah, an expert skier, plans to ski the most challenging mountains of Utah and Colorado in the coming winter. This climb is my big chance – my only chance. If I don't succeed there won't be another.

Crashing through an airborne jumble of rock and soil, burdened by intense fear and the pain of my shattering head, makes for a frenzied descent. *I can do this. I have to do this. I have to get home.* My compromised mind drifts back to fourteen years ago when a boating accident nearly killed me.

On a windy spring day on Long Island Sound, during a solo boat transfer, I was a mile from land when a misstep and a sudden wind shift hurled me into forty-five-degree water. I missed a spinning propeller by inches. Sinking immediately, I fought my way to the surface, discarding shoes and clothes while swallowing frigid salt water. The boat was gone. I was alone, and with my glasses lost I couldn't even be sure of the direction of the nearest land. Treading water while hoping for someone to find me would definitely result in freezing to death or drowning. Having no choice but to swim, I used a choppy, rough crawl stroke to head toward an indistinct shape in the distance that might have been the far-off hills of the Village at Sea Cliff.

Swimming through the sting of intense cold, I sensed that I wasn't alone. A comforting voice that seemed to envelop me kept repeating, in sync with my strokes: *If you don't quit, I won't leave you. If you don't quit, I won't leave you.* The voice provided comfort and strength. Focusing on this voice, I swam for half an hour, finally coming upon an anchored, abandoned boat several hundred yards from shore. Mustering the strength to pull myself onto the deck, I released the anchor line and drifted toward shore, naked and hypothermic, where rescue, hospital and home awaited.

Saved. . . but I should have died. I'll never know why I didn't. What miracle gave me the strength to swim through the cold and pain to return to my loved ones? I've never felt so close to God.

I don't know how I did it then, but now, high on this mountain, I believe in my soul that I can do it again.

White-necked raven. When we started seeing animals again
on the way down we knew we were nearing a safe altitude.

8

Descending

WE STUMBLE THROUGH the pebbly scree for hours toward Barafu Hut at 15,000 feet. We've passed quickly through the high alpine zone down to the low alpine zone; what took us a full night of climbing will take less than four hours coming down. We probably could have reached this point even sooner if we hadn't had to stop periodically for me to rest and breathe. I can get through this. I've survived worse. I will be with my family again.

Nearing more moderate altitudes, my eyesight begins to improve. We stop less frequently for me to fill up on oxygen. Then I smell food – what kind of food is anybody's guess, but I definitely smell food. Turns out, I'm not hallucinating; long before we see it we can tell we've arrived back at Barafu Hut. The longest four hours of my life are over.

The porters who remained here with our tents and gear, waiting for hours for the summit party's return, have prepared a meal of soup and rice and buttered bread. Tobias's plan is to stay at Barafu for less than an hour, break camp and then continue our descent. I breathe bottled oxygen, take more Decadron, and find a quiet place to rest for a few minutes. It's been seventy-eight hours since

I've slept, but with my head still pounding I fight to stay awake, convinced that falling asleep at 15,000 feet with cerebral edema will kill me. I will not and cannot under any circumstances fall asleep now. I dwell on the promise I made to my family to return safely. The medicine and oxygen must be helping, because I'm feeling some relief. We decide to continue down toward our planned destination of Mweka Camp – at 10,400 feet – a four-and-a-half-hour hike from Barafu.

Team Dirt is together again, and we're moving at a more manageable pace. As we descend, I peel off layers of clothing. The air gets denser and the terrain looks less like the moon and more like the rich green earth I hadn't even realized was absent at higher altitudes. The colors of the heather intensify. We pass running streams, and lush, beautiful vegetation found nowhere else in the world. At 12,500 feet we pass by the helicopter landing field at Millennium Camp, where a critically ill climber who's been carried or dragged down from the top of the mountain can be airlifted to a hospital in Arusha or Dar es Salaam. It doesn't seem possible, but I realize I haven't slept higher than the altitude I'm at right now; Shira Camp, four days ago, was at this exact elevation. I wonder if anyone else has ever completed a traditional seven-day climb of Kilimanjaro without having slept above 12,500 feet. But I'm walking down the mountain under my own power, with only 2,000 feet more to descend until camp and the possibility of safe sleep. The thought buoys me, filling my soul with confidence that I've made it this far, and I'm going to make it back safely on my own two feet. I didn't give up. I found the will to keep going and didn't quit.

Time and miles pass by and the pounding in my head subsides. I'm more alive with each passing hour. It's dusk when we finally reach Mweka Camp at 10,400 feet, after hiking for eighteen hours. In this one critical day we've climbed 4,400 feet to the summit, and then descended 9,000 feet.

Although I'm spent and exhausted, most symptoms of acute mountain sickness have subsided. On this sixth night, after eighty-five hours without sleep, I collapse in my tent, confident that sleep won't kill me: I probably won't stop breathing. The sleep that comes is deep and free of fear, like a child's. In the morning, the porters have to collapse my tent on top of me to wake me up.

Pushing beyond all limits, I finally reached a safe altitude to sleep for the first time in 85 hours, appearing and feeling as if I'd aged more than twenty years in seven days. I lost a dozen pounds in half as many days and needed months to fully recover from altitude sickness and exhaustion.

After breakfast on the morning of the seventh day, our twenty-six guides and porters, who cared for us on the mountain, sing Swahili songs to us. We shake their hands and thank them, using the few Swahili words and phrases we've learned over the past seven days on Mount Kilimanjaro: *Jambo Jambo Bwana. Hakuna Matata* (yes, really – *Hakuna Matata*). Together, we descend the final 5,000 feet to the base of the mountain.

On the morning of the seventh day on Mount Kilimanjaro
our guides and porters led by Tobias (left) and Goudance
(right) sang us traditional African songs before
accompanying us down to the base of the mountain.

9

Awakening

By MEANS OF real-time texts from Wendy and Sarah, Carol knew when we summited, and that I had altitude sickness. She waited another eight hours to hear directly from me that I'd made it down to Mweka Camp safely. Because of her long experience with my insomnia, she could imagine how sleeplessness on top of a mountain might have affected me. But it wasn't until some days after my return, when I gradually revealed the full details of my AMS and terrifying descent to safety, that she realized how, for a second time, she had almost lost me.

Hemingway wrote, *There's no one thing that's true. It's all true.* I unconsciously paid tribute to Hemingway by letting my truth come out in bits and pieces. It took some time for me to own up to the whole story of my experience on the mountain and my deception in withholding the true dangers prior to the climb.[1] While I sincerely promised to come down if I got sick, I didn't consider that sleeplessness should be included on the list of factors that would end my climb. I didn't account for pushing myself

---

[1] Until I was on my way back home from Africa, my parents thought I was on a two-week business trip to Belgium, where, for some unexplained reason, I was out of touch due to limited cell-phone service. I figured it was better to ask for forgiveness than permission. When they learned I was actually in Africa climbing Mount Kilimanjaro they were as mystified as when I told them, in my freshman year at Tulane, that I'd just jumped out of an airplane.

so hard to get to the top that I'd have absolutely nothing left for the descent. Every aspect of the trek was more difficult than I'd anticipated, and it took me months to fully recover.

After I returned, friends pressed me for minute details about my adventure. Most heard about the thrill and beauty of the climb; I focused on the end result more than the process of getting there, the way many women recall labor and delivery. Only a few were privy to more painful details. In more than one way, making it to the top of the mountain was one of my life's most significant achievements; the climb gave me a profound sense of fulfillment, although the quest itself was quixotic.

I know that climbing Kilimanjaro and putting all that I love at risk was a most imprudent ambition. Now, with the benefit of hindsight, I reflect on my time on the mountain. What's changed at home since I returned? What did I learn? I learned to pay better attention to my body's error messages. I learned that even the best-laid plans can go haywire. I planned and practiced and trained for many months, selected the most promising trekking company, and researched everything. I had every piece of equipment I could possibly need; I was as ready as I could possibly be to climb the tallest mountain in Africa. And yet, I nearly failed. I nearly died on that mountain because of something nobody predicted, but I should have anticipated: a total inability to sleep at high altitude that sapped my strength and almost did me in.

The Promise of Kilimanjaro

I know I broke the promises I made so confidently a half-year earlier. But, at the same time, I attained something that can't ever be taken away. While I wouldn't recommend that anyone tackle a mountain to climb out of a hole, that's exactly what I did. Because I was fortunate, it worked for me. I pushed myself beyond all limits and earned a personal success that carries forward in immeasurable ways in everything I now do. I put my demons in their place. In climbing to the top of Kilimanjaro, I was faithful to, and completed, my original mission. I saw that it was not just the mountain I conquered, but also myself.

This is and will always be with me – and it gives me pause. I've often replayed the moment of decision, behind the shelter of the giant rocks, with eyes swollen shut, in the howling wind just after sunrise at Stella Point. This was when I could have, and should have, told Tobias, *I'm giving up.* Looking back now, even with the knowledge of the pain and danger that soon followed, would I still have chosen to go on? Or, would I have quit – just an hour from the summit? Honestly, I don't know.

Was Hemingway's leopard following a false scent when he became lost at such a high altitude? Or, in making it to the top of Mount Kilimanjaro, was he fulfilling his own destiny? Unlike the leopard, I *could* explain why I climbed the mountain and why I *had* to return home. I'm comforted knowing that family and friends prayed for my safety, sent me strength during the endless nights, and helped will me up, and back down, the mountain. New friends who climbed with me knew what to do when things went wrong. I always knew I wasn't alone. I'm grateful that I made it up and down the mountain under my own power. I'm grateful that I got to complete my climb before the snows of Kilimanjaro are gone forever. I'm grateful that I made it home. I've reconfirmed how much more valuable my family is to me than the pursuit of pure adventure. I've recovered the passion for my work that had eluded me during and after my illnesses. Most of all, I'm grateful for my health, so that I can continue to be present for Carol and be a positive force in the lives of our daughters and their growing families. Knowing all of this helps keep the spring in my step.

As for my continued athletic pursuits, they're more frequent but far less ambitious. I've climbed Mount Washington and biked the Great Allegheny Passage. Carol and I walk for hours everywhere we travel, and still love sailing on Long Island Sound. Someday I hope to walk one hundred miles from the Irish Sea to the North Sea, along Hadrian's Wall in Northern England; here the greatest danger would be choking on a power bar.

As I look back on the adventure of my lifetime, I'm proud to have stood for one brief moment on the summit of Mount Kilimanjaro. This is enough for me; there's nothing left to prove. Since Kilimanjaro, I've seen my three daughters grow into beautiful women. I've walked two of them down the aisle, and Carol and I are now grandparents. How close did I come to missing all of this? I could never again put my life at risk to pursue what, in retrospect, was a selfish endeavor, and I'm very much at peace with not becoming the explorer of my dreams.

WHEN WE REACHED the Mweka Gate at the foot of Kilimanjaro we were trucked back to our hotel in Moshi, Tanzania, where I reconnected with Patience to pick up the Tanzanite stone I'd chosen for Carol. Now, when she wears her beautiful necklace, she knows it represents the most important promise, the one I made to her at the airport before leaving for Africa, the promise I kept: I came home to her.

The Promise of Kilimanjaro

ONE DAY, ABOUT a year after returning from Kilimanjaro, I showed Carol an article about climbing the Matterhorn. Nestled in the Alps, on the border of Switzerland and Italy, near the town of Zermatt, the Matterhorn has a summit of less than 14,700 feet. While the Matterhorn doesn't present the risk of extreme altitude, climbing the rocky Swiss mountain requires climbers and guides to be tied together with safety ropes to avoid falling off the summit ridge.

What do you think? I asked.

You know, Jay, Carol said, *I used to be the* **yes** *wife. Now I'm the* **no** *wife.*

I know, I said. *I was just making sure.*

Jay Scheiner

With Carol

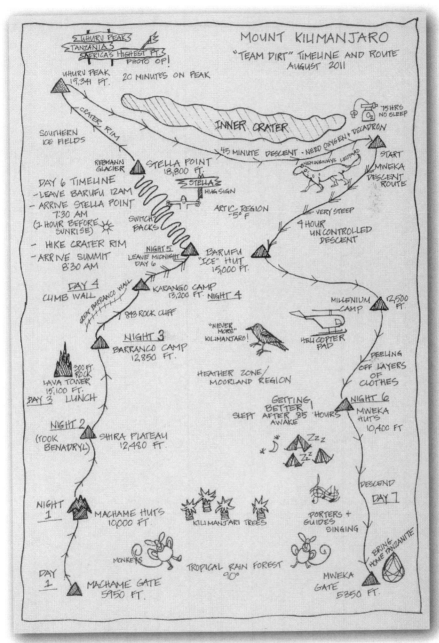

Team Dirt's timeline and route on Mount Kilimanjaro, August 2011

Acknowledgments

I wish to express my gratitude to my editor, Sharyn Essman. Sharyn helped bring this story to life, giving me assignments and forcing me to dig ever deeper to reveal exactly what happened each day on the mountain, and what led me to want to climb Kilimanjaro in the first place. She took many of my raw sentences and refined them, while coordinating design, layout, and photo placement. Thank you, Sharyn, for the year you spent living with the story, and I appreciate how much you cared about the process and final outcome. Thanks to Izzy Essman for your production skills as assistant to the editor.

I'd like to thank my climbing partners, Wendy Swart, Sarah Lewis Marino and Larry Wood, for their friendship and support during our time on the mountain, and especially during the trials of the descent.

All of the photographs on Mount Kilimanjaro were taken by Wendy Swart, Sarah Lewis Marino, or by me. The Tanzanite necklace was photographed by Carlos Valencia.

Thank you Amy Klein for the beautiful, hand-drawn maps of Kilimanjaro, and for illustrating Team Dirt's ascent to the summit and return.

Jay Scheiner

Thank you Brian Gertler for your technical expertise and initial designs for the wraparound cover.

Joseph Jordan – I appreciate your thoughtful Forward. Each day I try to live up to the ideals outlined in your book, *Living a Life of Significance*. Thank you for continuing to remind me of the role the life insurance profession plays in helping to keep families and businesses together when tragedy occurs, and protecting clients' financial security when they become ill.

Deepest thanks to Ash Tewari for guiding me through the course of treatment for my prostate cancer, curing me through his skilled surgery, and for inspiring me to climb the mountain. I am forever grateful to you. I also wish to thank the team of cardiologists, nurses and staff at New York University Medical Center for their successful treatment of my a-fib/SVT.

Many thanks to my business partners and friends at Agent Support Group who rooted for me and helped keep things humming while I was training and away in Africa.

As my late father, Murray Scheiner, would say, I have gold – three very special daughters: Jessica Kotkin, Rebecca Henick and Marissa Scheiner. To my golden daughters: thank you for always being there in every way and special thanks for finally approving a picture of the three of you that I was permitted to include in this book.

With daughters Jessica, Rebecca & Marissa in 2016, five years
after climbing Mount Kilimanjaro. I had a lot to lose.

Carol, the dedication page says it all…

Resources

Aeppel, T. "Taking on 'Everyman's Everest.'" *The Wall Street Journal* 23-24 July 2011: D10. Print.

- Excellent primer on climbing Kilimanjaro that was published just a week before I left for Africa to climb the great mountain. He pointed out that as one of the most attainable of the world's highest mountains, Kilimanjaro can be ascended without sophisticated mountaineering equipment or skills. Aeppel also describes how and why the mountain's challenges are often underestimated.

Archer, J. *Paths of Glory*. St. Martin's Press, 2009. Print.

- Historical fiction about the great mountain climber George Mallory. It was Mallory who, when asked why he was climbing Mount Everest, stated famously, *because it's there.* Reading about Mallory reminded me that the most important thing was for me to make it back home from Mount Kilimanjaro. His frozen, mummified body was found on Mount Everest 75 years after he and his climbing partner disappeared on the mountain. I had every intention of returning home safely from my Africa adventure.
- It was George Mallory who said, *Have we vanquished an enemy? None but ourselves.* This quote was later misattributed to Sir Edmund Hillary, who had changed it to, *It*

is not the mountain we conquer, but ourselves. I've further modified the phrase to: *I saw that it was not just the mountain I conquered, but also myself.*

Clarke, L. (2010, December 12). *Martina Navratilova Reflects on her Attempt to Climb Mount Kilimanjaro.* Retreived from http://www.washingtonpost.com/wp-dyn/content/article/2010/12/12/ AR2010121202730.html?tid=nn_twitter.

- Ms. Navratilova is an amazing woman and an inspiration. *The trek, she said, was the most physically and mentally demanding thing she had ever been through, made in the face of unrelenting rain that turned to snow on Day Two – conditions the local guides and porters who accompanied the 27 hikers described as the worst they'd seen on the mountain...* 'I've always said, "The only failure is when you fail to try,' Navratilova said. 'The other failure would be not giving your best effort. And I feel I did both: I tried and gave my very best effort. It just wasn't meant to be.' Navratilova undertook the challenge less than two months after undergoing radiation for a non-invasive form of breast cancer.*

Dorr, D. *Kissing Kilimanjaro: Leaving It All on Top of Africa.* Mountaineers Books, 2010. Print.

- Engaging book about the author's two attempts to climb the mountain, including stories of the interesting personalities, climbers and guides he met along the way. He gave it all to fight altitude sickness and summited on his second attempt.

Graham, Robin Lee. *Dove*. Harper Collins, 1972. Print.

- Robin, my boyhood hero, sailed around the world alone on his sloop, the *Dove*.

Hemingway, Ernest. "The Snows of Kilimanjaro." *The Snows of Kilimanjaro and Other Stories*. Charles Scribner's Sons, 1961. Print.

- Hemingway has been credited with the quote about the only real sports being bullfighting and mountain climbing. The quote actually comes from Barnaby Conrad, a contemporary of Hemingway's who was an actual bullfighter, as well as bon vivant, writer and restaurateur. The full quote is generally accepted as: "Only bullfighting, mountain climbing and auto racing are sports, the rest are merely games."

Jordan, Joseph W. *Living a Life of Significance*. Acanthus Publishing, 2013. Print.

- Joseph Jordan's philosophy regarding my profession inspires me and brings insight into my career. Jordan says, *By providing people with independence, dignity, and a legacy, you are part of the noblest profession in the world.*

Kilimanjaro Climbing Details. Tusker Trail, 2011. Print.

- This is a go-to source and checklist for anyone thinking of climbing Kilimanjaro. I quoted some on-point language from the guidebook. Tusker Trail is a respected trekking organization founded by Eddie Frank, one of the foremost authorities on Mount Kilimanjaro and has climbed the mountain over 50 times. The manual contains excellent information including descriptions of all major ascent routes, including the seven-day Machame Route. It also outlines the equipment, clothing, immunizations, medications and training regimen required for climbing Kilimanjaro.

Kilimanjaro: To the Roof of Africa. Dir. David Brashears. The National Geographic Society, 2000. Film.

- This video follows a diverse group of climbers and their guide up Africa's tallest mountain. Although a little corny, it's beautifully made, and during my preparations for climbing the mountain I watched it over and over.

Lawrence, T.E., *The Seven Pillars of Wisdom.* Wordsworth Classics of World Literature, 1999. Print.

- The story of the real Lawrence of Arabia. In poetic terms, he describes a life of adventure and purpose during his time helping unify Arab groups against the occupying

Turkish army during World War One. I used this source for the quote about the *dreamer of the day.*

Meyer, Hans. *Across East African Glaciers: An Account of the First Ascent of Kilimanjaro.* Trans. E.H.S. Calder. Whitefish, MT: Kessinger Publications, 2007 (originally published in German in 1890). Print.

- The story of what it took to be the first man to stand on the roof of Africa. The science and the knowledge Meyer brought to the world was remarkable. His successful ascent with partner Ludwig Purtscheller was immeasurably more difficult than it is today – no groomed trails, no cleared forest, an almost impenetrable ice barrier covered the entire top of the mountain. Meyer was a great explorer.

Moore, T. (2003, February 16). *Kilimanjaro? Well, It Nearly Killed Me.* Retrieved from https://www.theguardian.com/travel/2003/feb/16/tanzania.climbingholidays.observerescapesection.

- *It was universally agreed that here was the most appalling voluntary activity one could undertake in peacetime, the worst thing anyone with a compact zoom round their neck could ever pay to do. I proposed a high six-figure sum in sterling when debating what financial inducement could persuade us to turn round and do it again, and proved comfortably the lowest bidder.*

Moushabeck, M. & Schulz, H. *Kilimanjaro: A Photographic Journey to the Roof of Africa*, Interlink Books, 2011. Print.

- Stunning photographs of terrain and plant life and vivid descriptions of the mountain and of summiting Kilimanjaro. Authors, a husband and wife, climbed the mountain together and fully documented their climb.

Reader, John. *Africa: A Biography of the Continent*, New York: Vintage, 1999.

Rimoch, D. & Cherng, S. (2013, December 20). *A Rare and Beautiful Stone Fails to Shine: Tanzania's Missed Opportunity.* Retrieved from http://knowledge.wharton.upenn.edu/article/ rare-beautiful-stone-fails-shine-tanzanias-missed-opportunity

Scheiner, Jay. "Overboard Alone." *Yachting Magazine*, 62-66, September 1997. Print.

- The account of my improbable survival after falling off a moving boat while alone on Long Island Sound.

The Snows of Kilimanjaro. Dir. Henry King. Twentieth Century Fox, 1961. Film.

- Based on Hemingway's 1936 short story, the film stars Gregory Peck, Ava Gardner and Susan Hayward. The film version is expanded to include many true aspects of Hemingway's life. In the film, a bartender suggests that the leopard ended up atop Kilimanjaro as he followed a false scent and became lost. Nobody knows the real story.

Stedman, H., *Kilimanjaro: The Trekking Guide to Africa's Highest Mountain* (3rd ed.) Trailblazer Publications, 2010. Print.

- This is *the* famous trekking guide – my bible for preparing to climb the mountain. I felt it was so important as a reference that I carried it with me in my day pack during the first half of the climb and tore out and threw away chapters to lighten my pack as I reached the real-life milestones. It's a valuable book to have even if you have no intention of climbing Kilimanjaro.
- Stedman vividly describes the beautiful plant-life on the mountain, including the giant tree groundsel, or Senecio trees, and Lobelia deckenii flowers.
- Stedman describes the descent route involving switchbacks as easier on both nerves and knees vs. the more direct upper descent route on the Mweka trail.

Stewart, A., *Kilimanjaro: A Complete Trekker's Guide*, Cicerone Press Limited, 2012. Print.

- Basic trekking guide and a good general reference.

The Wildest Dream: Conquest of Everest, 2010.

- National Geographic documentary film about George Mallory, obsessed with becoming the first climber to summit Mount Everest, who disappeared on Everest in 1924 with his climbing partner Andrew Irvine. The film intertwines two stories, one about climber Conrad Anker, who discovered Mallory's body on Everest in 1999. Anker returned to Everest to try to duplicate Mallory's climb using traditional 1920's technology and clothing. We will never know if Mallory and Irvine were the first to stand on Everest's summit. A beautiful film.

About the author

Jay Scheiner is a partner at Agent Support Group, a New York-based brokerage firm specializing in providing life insurance planning solutions for families and businesses. Jay's writing on financial services and human interest has been featured in a variety of publications, among them Broker World and Yachting Magazine.

After graduating from law school, Jay served in federal law enforcement before entering the financial services industry. He holds a U.S. Coast Guard Captain's License and a black-belt in Shotokan Karate. He climbed Mount Kilimanjaro in August,

2011. Jay and his wife, Carol, live in Manhasset, Long Island. This is Jay's first book.

If you would like to know more about *The Promise of Kilimanjaro*, visit www.thepromiseofkilimanjaro.com.

Made in the USA
Columbia, SC
17 April 2018